A Wintry Rebirth

Gabrielle Creque

BookLeaf
Publishing

India | USA | UK

A Wintry Rebirth © 2022 Gabrielle Creque

All rights reserved.

No part of this publication may be reproduced, stored in a retrieval system, or transmitted, in any form or by any means, electronic, mechanical, photocopying, recording or otherwise, without the prior written permission of the presenters.

Gabrielle Creque asserts the moral right to be identified as author of this work.

Presentation by *BookLeaf Publishing*

Web: www.bookleafpub.com

E-mail: info@bookleafpub.com

ISBN: 9789357215046

First edition 2022

*My first book is dedicated to my sister
Danielle who offered tremendous help and
encouragement along my journey.*

PREFACE

These poems were written with a short 25 years of experience under my belt. I was assigned female at birth but struggled all my life with my identity. My idea of who I am does not fit my actual image. Still I persist in having my voice heard and my feelings expressed. I acknowledge there is much left to see, hear and feel. These ideas have not fully matured but I will stay true to my journey and await my hopefully golden years.

Wintry

My current journey has been wearisome
I am less than halfway there
Echoes of emptiness, tired and tiresome
But it is never ending my dear

I run and hear the crackle of ice
I don't feel it is slippery
Winter is dangerous, glittery, filled with strife
I fought winter with all my might

At home I am blanketed in warmth
I consume it, heating me from inside out
I am still dissatisfied, I am still torn
My lone hot drink pouring forth

More time than I need in these seventeen hour
nights
In comfortable darkness there is artificial light
In standing against this, I cannot win every fight
Hopelessness, among other things, fills my sight

Long nights can bring shimmering skies
Looking up at this view, tiring to wonder why
Uncertainty lingers then vulnerability is nigh
Chaos ensues, no choice but to take it in stride

Entertainment

This media serves only to make us docile
With these leaders we can never reconcile
Forced conformity through theft of free will
Limited by the narrow path of survival

He who poisoned the river has fish for sale
Then gives me the 'choice', starve or eat
From the summit of his profit, he cannot hear
the wails
With the knowledge he'll otherwise fail, he cries
"Join me"

Distracted by your own likeness on display
Deepest desires revealed by coveted content
Your attention is held but no interest in what
they say
Carefully concocted traps, no matter your intent

Break free from this brainwashing
It serves only to divide and conquer us
Our unity is wavering
I must fight against my conqueror

Cosmic Dust

The iron in my blood has travelled quite a
distance
Particles of the stars form my resistance
I simply watch the cosmic dust dance
Seeing clouds of smoke as I slip into a trance

My racing mind, I lay awake
Numb to the pain, internal wounds are not the
same
I pray to God my soul to take
It was all in vain, wild desires never tamed

My healing is temporary, I was never whole
Constant torture remove all hope
Consistent danger reminds me I stand alone
My wounds reopen because of the seeds I've
sown

My cosmic dust will journey further
One life ends, reborn as another
In time I'll be completely shattered
Still start anew like nothing mattered

Repetition

I watch the sun rise
Through clouded view of the skies
I have not done it all yet
Again I watch the sun set

I watch the sun rise
I still await my demise
I must be productive, I cannot forget
Again I watch the sun set

I watch the sun rise
I've not succeeded after many tries
Nostalgia is my drug, I must reflect
Again I watch the sun set

I watch the sun rise
Still here to my surprise
Cleanse my mind after I have wept
Again I watch the sun set

I watch the sun rise
When I conform there is no prize
Internal vengeance for past regrets
Again I watch the sun set

I watch the sun rise
Unable to see clearly through my lies
I have no choice but to place my bet
Again I watch the sun set

Time

Alone I walk in misty mornings
Going as long as I can without mourning
Burying and hiding my longing
I am Hollow, After Dark I turn Into Nothing

Sully not your pride for the sake of your needs
You will turn dry along with your seeds
Sidetracked but still perform good deeds
Pushed and pulled until your soul bleeds

To survive this wretched world so cruel
Embrace each day, win every duel
Pity it's impossible says the fool
If you fail and fail again, go back to school

An extensive task to build this ploy
What if there's nothing to enjoy?
See the world! Explore foreign soil!
My location might change but I still toil

Toil hard and long for no reward
Stay in your place and respect your Lord
Be grateful for what little you have now
Stay on the path, wanderers are not allowed

The Meaning of Life

I am not searching for purpose
In this existence I have no compass
If a God is out there, someone would save us
I am empty of all faith and trust

Maybe we should enjoy the simple breezy air
Or we should spread joy and cheer
Why can't we just happen to be here?
We might be in search of nothing I fear

Magnetism too strong to be mere coincidence
These beliefs serve as a strong defence
Unopened minds save no space for resilience
Disprove it and they shatter so tense

Anything is possible but some things unlikely
We follow our own laws to control the psyche
Crossing paths with the most timely
Nothing is concrete, we must forge destiny

Angry at the Self

Untethered rage leaves a lingering lust for blood
Even if the blade is pointed at oneself
Unfulfilled desire follows me on my trod
Life moves forward without me; only time will
tell

My anger is heard but my words forgotten
Stagnant irritation makes my soul rotten
Bottling it up makes my mind molten
There is no salvation for the fallen

Memories burned in so my grudge holds true
I create my path in spite of what I do
In this life I only do what I have to
Time heals all wounds except you

Forgive and forget; easier said than done
My guardians gave up, I came undone
Must be nice to have crimes so easily forgotten
Or maybe these crimes are a product of my
imagination

When I'm finally alone, the memories will soften
With time and experience I won't be sullen
Cold blade pointed at me withdrawn

There will be no more raging storms

9

Frustration

Awake again with the same day on repeat
A new day with the same tasks to complete
I would rather lay the day to waste
Than respond to the voices in my robotic state

Awake again with the same song on repeat
Even in recreation my thoughts still bleak
This repetitive life makes me weak
I bottle it up but my frustration leaks

Awake again with the same thought on repeat
After frustration comes my defeat
I have no choice but to self-destruct
Even though I am moving, I feel stuck

Awake again with the same haze on repeat
From this repetition a change I seek
Today looks the same, hopelessness peaked
Unable to break free, I go to sleep

At Night

Gazing upon these stars so dim
Thinking of his eyes so bright
I only dream of caressing him
In his absence I don't feel right
We meet again and I feel at home
In empty streets we own the night
Privileged to have your hand to hold
Together our spark makes fire ignite
Your soul whispers sweetly to mine
A conversation full of wonder
Endless moments intertwined
I will never love another
Heart on my sleeve; I am laid bare
After dusk the most playful pair

Strayed Stranger

No desire to live, no desire to die
Lost in my dreams, I wandered too high
I could leave behind this life full of sighs
Fighting all our lives to be recognised
Should I believe when they say love is the prize?
Through hoops of fire is where your lover lies
Scorched, burned, yet to see it with these eyes
On my knees, I have lost and cut all ties
When will I realise I believed lies?
Deafening screams but no one hears my cries
At least I can say I really tried
We got old but haven't yet got wise
I'll turn to dust and soar through the sky
There was no real me, only the disguise

Awaiting Death

I dreamt of death again last night
He told me he couldn't take me today
I know I will wake up to that dreadful site
He told me I am here to stay

I find myself envious of those who die young
When it seems like my fire will never burn out
I curse at everyone with venomous tongue
There is nothing else I'm passionate about

The end of time draws nearer each minute
Unorthodox desire to die, how do I kill it?
At night Death says to me in dreams so vivid
"You will never be complete, you are too timid"

Nothing and no one makes the desire go away
I cannot die, I cannot be free from this fate
Punished with life, empty of all hope
Eventually I will reach the end of my rope

When I get there I'll have nothing to show
Naught but sadness, my mind sunk below
I take comfort in Death's cold embrace
My life disappeared without a trace

A Mistake called Life

My heart beats but I am dead inside
No need to eat, waiting to collide
With my last breath time holds us apart
A long life lived, a bitter taste from the start

They were misunderstood but the seed's still
sown
My parents confront their mistakes now I am
grown
As I suspected they seem not to care
When I confront their mistakes, everything is
unclear

We are not complex people
By our nature we are peaceful
Checkered pasts behind, untold futures ahead
I will find my way after being misled

Hidden away the scars of my past
The present is now and happening fast
The day of my birth this curse was cast
Bound to my breath for as long as the days last

Society's Destruction

15

After the dust settles to the ground
Desolation is in the air all around
Ashen expressions now eternal
Any certainty is now ephemeral

Powerful people passed down this punishment
Nothing remains; we must rebuild
Within confines of our new management
Death by complacency; our futures were killed

Too satisfied with our perfect lives
The suffering we chose not to see
Too distracted to see our looming demise
No one takes responsibility for a failed
community

Creation

Take anything as inspiration
Everything has a beautiful story
Even a tragic start ends in wondrous creation
Humble products of our minds seek not glory

Divinity and wonder draw me in so magnetic
The light of curiosity is never diminished
Infinite possibilities make me mesmeric
True creators know our work is never finished

Longing

I lost my clarity a long time ago
Internal fear and panic but don't let it show
Oh, how I wish I could let the past go
Oh, what could've been I will never know

Very tempted to run away again
But there will always be another mountain
Rejection awaits and it is stifling
Try and try again but the pain is crippling

Happiness continues to elude me
Oh frantic mind, please let me be!
I lay awake to watch the shadows creep
My patience thinning, it's plain to see

Time moves forward but I am still
I was getting by, up until
I was told to give it some more time
Wanting something this much should be a crime

The real pain is just under my skin
I'll enjoy your virtual company within
I can be a friend if that is allowed
Cannot let my noisy thoughts take me down

Wanderer

There is wonder in being alone
Freedom is within our grasp or so I am told
Not much has changed now I am grown
There is still no place to call home

Compelled to go against the grain
Nothing to lose, nothing to gain
Unable to live any other way
I tried to conform but now it's too late

It will come to an end in time
My wander through this mysterious life
Nomad tales to end the night
Start anew with the dawn's light

No Saviour

19

Take time to seek solace
Self soothing is only natural
Drowning my view of the distant surface
In healing I'll learn to excel

The burdens we carry
Are bore by no other
Doubts must be buried
We are pledged to go further

Shadows lurk within Godless existence
Our saviour is lost in a world so vast
Do not will yourself to be so tense
We create our salvation; so stay steadfast

Hope

My resolution to improve
Hand in hand with kindness
Strive to make mountains move
Make my way out of the wilderness

Planning anything can be considered brave
Because our plans cannot escape change
Shaping the future is the noble aim
We must usher in the new age

Stay focused and trust your process
Fulfil your fated tasks around town
Stay true to oneself, potential is boundless
Where faith was lost, hope can be found